Eve Would Know

Eve Would Know

Poems by
Joanne Leva

Kelsay Books

Cover: Eric Medlin
Author Photograph: David Gilleece

ISBN 13-978-1-945752-62-9

Kelsay Books
Aldrich Press
www.kelsaybooks.com

For Christopher Bursk

Acknowledgments

I admire and loved working with the Montgomery County Poet Laureate (MCPL) Celebrity Judges: Sonia Sanchez, Robert Pinsky, Robert Hass, Gerald Stern, Gregory Orr, Ellen Bryant Voigt, Grace Paley, Galway Kinnell, Carolyn Forche, Marie Howe, Tony Hoagland, Robert Bly, Christopher Bursk, Kathleen Sheeder Bonanno, Ethel Rackin, J.C. Todd, Major Jackson, Carl Dennis, and Tim Seibles. Thank you for being so wonderful to me.

I owe so much to the MCPLs: Yolanda Wisher, Margaret Almon, Deidra Greenleaf Allan, Jon Volkmer, Nicole Greaves, Teresa Mendez-Quigley, Sean Webb, Deborah Fries, David Simpson, Elizabeth Rivers, Doris Ferleger, Grant Clauser, Amy Small-McKinney, Liz Chang, Glenn McLaughlin, Kristina Moriconi, David Escobar-Martin, Autumn Konopka, and Chad Frame.

And thank you to all my friends who inspire me: Eric Medlin, Fran Baird, Jim Fillman, Marilyn Gross, Steve Pollack, Rodger Lowenthal, Joe Tice, Hayden Saunier, Susan Charkes, Helen Mirkil, Brian Peterson, Tom Mallouk, Bernadette McBride, Terry Culleton, Peter Krok, Leonard Gontarek, Lorraine Henrie Lins, Matilda Bray, Paul Siegell, Louisa Schnaithmann, Luray Gross, Carla Spataro, Christine Weiser, Courtney Bambrick, Marshall Warfield, Thomas Dooley, Michael Parrish, Adrian Todd Zuniga, Laren McClung, David Kime, Cleveland Wall, Elise Brand, Joanne Coppens, Joe Chelius, Brigette Erwin, Michelle Greer, and David Gilleece.

But most of all, I want to thank two very important people: my adorable daughter, Julie Anne Schoettle, for always believing in me; and my sweet husband, John Mosemann, for being such a constant, gentle spirit.

I would like to thank the following literary anthology in whose pages the poem, "Eve Strives to Become an Opera Singer," first appeared: 50 Over Fifty (PS Books, 2016).

I would also like to thank the following magazine for including some of the work found here: Transcendent Visions.

Contents

Trouble in Paradise

Man Driving with One Hand on the Wheel

Eve Pollinates the Flower of Love

Innocence Lost

Eve Calls the Motor Club Man to Recharge Her Battery

Trouble in Paradise

The Original Flaw

Adam puts his hand
in his pants pocket.
There is a large bulge.
He becomes confined by fear.

First Days and Nights in Paradise

Eve accepts her strange fate.

Picture a dark
candlelit restaurant.
Sitting across from Adam
acting exactly like the woman
he wants her to be,
Eve whispers to herself,

He's perfect.

Tip of Iceberg

Adam, an avid
fisherman, surprises Eve
by taking her fishing.

He hands her his pole
and waits until she notices
it isn't dangling over the side.

Home Team

Adam dreams of hitting
a home run
in the ninth inning

of the last game
of the World Series,
or scoring the winning touchdown

in the final seconds.
Eve reads gossip sheets
and delays her plans.

Adam's Desire

As if out of prison
Adam comes home horny.
Eve wears a negligee,
scribbles with a gloved finger, *I love you,*
on the bathroom mirror.

His fantasy—
a seductive dance
when he walks
in the door.
Kingdom come.

Great Dividends

Eve understands
and Adam appreciates.

He takes her to a flower show,
buys her roses

in whatever vase she wants;
the production,

the hair net,
and realm of possibility.

Puff Balls

To liberate
chaos into clouds
of spores

is like studying
the creation
between 3 and 5 in the afternoon.

She Recreates

Adam is horny. Again.
Eve wears a negligee.

She dances
a seductive dance.

He experiences love
like a cherry on a sundae.

Fall in or Out of It

Adam is a performer.
The first man–truly
a coveted position
bestowed upon him
by decoded melodies
from the King.

It is a dramatic walk
like passing a storefront
a color catches your eye
you turn to look back.

The virtual marriage,
like a hat on a mannequin.
They create.
They hunt.
Toil and embark
on an everlasting journey.

No one is certain
if all of the animals
from the Ark
joined the wedding march,
but fumes from past rendezvous

permeated as Adam
looked on.

Eve, escorted
by the north wind,
blew down the aisle.
Giraffes, pigs, and geese

followed in unison
two-by-two.
Eve curtsied.
Adam bowed

and reflected with nepotism:
As I venture into this garden
the grass kisses my feet
each dandelion grows

to cushion my stride.
There could be a bed
of honeysuckle
but that isn't how it goes.

Now we're dead.

Exit here. Enter there.
Terminate when the surface
is less firm.

Wake me when it's over.

It's over.
Eve stands beside him
longing for his touch
nothing but stage lights.

Scurry to white noise.
Shoulder snap.
Hair toss to the side.
Lips start.

Voices expand and contract.
Keep your pretty chin up.
Eve questions.
She sees Adam stare.
She studies his face,
his walk, his ways.
She wanders in card stores,
suggests coffee,
imagines making love
under pool tables,
in station wagons
and making his food.

At this point,
a miracle happens.

Adam embraces the evening.
He uses extravagant phrases
undaunted by perspiring.

He says,
let's poke around
among the wreckage.
We may discover golden clams
in what seems to be ruin.
Scallops swim
where bliss surrounds them
and Eve reaches
beyond herself.
She delivers newspapers
to hostages
and rolls tobacco
cigarettes.

Adam holds a snake.
It's a large one
inoffensive and rather
beautiful just the same.

He asks Eve to take it
and she is grateful,
she supposes.

Good in Greenhouse

Save a few seed heads
for the birds, but keep the rest
for the fall from grace.

Endowed with Perfection

Adam discharges
his origin and gazes

toward the vanishing point.
He shakes off the earth,

twining stems, and leaves
round and deeply lobed,

fragrance strong.
There is great joy

and lovely bedding
in the late-fall garden.

Holes of nothingness
open up like an eclipse.

In half sun and half shade,
orange pod-like lanterns

lie in horizontal position.
Their berries droop

with each change
of the moon.

There Are Encounters and There Are
Detective Stories

Eve's spiritual qualities
and her need for understanding
send her once again,

in one crooked direction.
The emergence
of her private life

to the stage
keeps her locked,
in a vicious cycle

of private eye drama.
Eve's latest discovery:
dramatizing convoluted marital scenes.

Especially sweet-scented
at dusk and evening,
a sweep of blooms

and charming seedpods
trigger a fountain of reminiscences.
She recounts wild dreams

in vignettes and sketches.
Her story designed by a mind alive,
clairvoyant.

Bystander

It is midnight and raining.
Eve's unblinking eyes
stream with tears,

forever before her
the Parrish-blue sky
burlesquing.

The same place.
The next day
the story ends

where it began.
The emptiness
of the garden

may be glimpsed.
The curtain rises
on her bare body

bathed in gray light.
A whistle hangs
from her neck.

Three Views of a Molt

Eyes open.
Face buried among the folds
of body.
Snake moves in
direct contact with the ground,
sensitive to faint vibrations.
Complete disintegration
into nothingness.

Eyes cloud.
Old skin liquefies
and separates from the new
skin beneath.
Belly scales grip terrain,
its shuck now dull and spiritless.
A misty sea of dye and rouge
quivers in air.

Eyes clear.
Snake crawls out.
The cast skin peels
backward from head to tail
leaving an empty husk.
To emerge
like blue flowers against a silvery
mottled moon.

Sunday in the Garden

When songbirds begin
their serenades
in towering gum trees,

and woodpeckers mark
their territory
with tap and drum,

look for turtles and frogs
sunning themselves
by the water's edge.

As evening approaches,
search the sky
for hawks,

the creek for ducks.
Watch dragonflies swarm
and turkey vultures soar.

Back Home

An unconventional rehearsal.
Adam has taken tango lessons,
dazzles everyone with his moves.

A misty rain lasts
until the photographer
shows up desperate and hungry.

Eve runs into an old friend.
They celebrate
with a pitcher of lemon fizz.

Trouble in Paradise

Eve is attuned
to Adam's cruelly
self-serving cues.

Their relationship seems on
its last legs.
Foreplay becomes non-existent

after sex cuddling
dwindles.
Adam makes excuses.

He struggles with the grass.
Maybe it is greener
on the other side?

Man Driving with One Hand on the Wheel

Nude Descending Staircase

A motionless form
folds into an untidy
slip cover
on the living
room sofa.

Her left arm
and left leg
lie like the dark
blue rug. Her figure
flattened

by my father's
crushing abandon.
In my about
out-grown night
gown, as if

naked, I
descend the staircase
with girlish
prudence. but barely
advance.

Man Driving with One Hand on the Wheel

Sitting in the loathsome
back of the vintage
gold-metal Chevy
convertible,
I am compliant

as they fight for the
coveted front seat
next to our celebrity-like
once-a-month dad.

When settled in our
sameness, an air of
nonchalance coalesces
and his deliberate arm
dangles down.

Sacred Sestina

I never thought my breath would come to sex.
Like a disowned child or an abortion,
the heartache of rape never leaves.
I can hardly speak of the fire-engine-red
flags in my head, when I am alone at night.
The moon waxes. Its crescent swell shows in the sky.

I trace the various groupings of stars in the sky
with my thumb. Sometimes I wish on one for sex.
But most of the time, it's a lonely night.
My desire has been removed like an abortion.
And my love, the bloody clot of consciousness, drops into a pool
    of red.
My child grows up, grows out and leaves.

I remember being 9 years old, when my father left.
I used to rest my head in my hands and look up to the sky.
Those summer days drug by. Burning hot, I became the cold,
    cold night.
I spent my time trying to be good at sex,
performing like a whore's child. I bled.
Left alone, looking for the light in the dark, dark drape

of night. If I could, I would re-write those curtains,
make them windows instead. I would write out the silence that
    was left
and the black sky.
I wish for a boozy abortion!
Make it maroon!
And forsake my sex!

I guess there are worse things than intoxicated sex,
people who smother you, like smoke in the night.
I sense arrival after an ordinary flush.
The struggle to keep a child from leaving—
to purge like a shooting star streaking across the arc of sky.
What is left in the end is flesh.

Why is love red?
What color is sex?

How does the sky
release the night?
And who is left
after the transformation?

There is no innocence in sex after the destruction.
The book of body has already been read.
The wide sky delivers the hard flame of night.

Memory of the VFW in Glenside

It's the third Sunday,
once again, we end up at the bar.

Dad slowly inserts his card-key and an
ominous buzz unlocks the door.

Bodies flicker in filament from the midday sun
playing peekaboo through venetian blinds.

First Kiss

Complex laundry
room lint face.
Six of us sit

on washers and dryers.
An empty Budweiser
bottle spins

on the cement grey floor,
stops at me.
Open lips cock.

Eve Pollinates the Flower of Love

Eve Begins the Day Missing Mass

God: You can leave now.
Adam: All right, damn it, we'll go.
Eve: Good-bye.
Adam: Is that all you can say—just good-bye?

Eve: See ya, sailor.
Adam: Go to hell.

One Giant Step Past Blame

With the flick of an eyebrow
and a dose of grace,

there is a kind
of holiness

in the air and an innocent
breeze through the window.

Adam and Eve penetrate
the fabric of their skins.

As each fig leaf falls,
it is followed by the next, then the next, then the next.

Eve Becomes a Bohemian

"It's the dab of grit that seeps into an oyster's shell that makes the pearl, not pearl-making seminars with other oysters."

—Stephen King

After being thrown in the gutter
and flattened out,

her uncreated moments
appear in a column of indigo smoke.

The marble kitchen sink
sterilizes dinner dishes.

A bland sentence
takes a quick turn and purifies.

Eve seeks to be soaked,
craves to be clean again.

The Pure and Terrible

Looking back,
Eve has no regrets.

There are always
catastrophes.

The stripping down
to barebones.

To swing
by a courthouse

then straight for the airport
stopping only to drop tears

and announcement cards
in the mailbox.

Young lovers cry their loss,
they have some explaining.

Adjoining Gardens

Eve stands in front
of a full-length mirror
and imagines talking to Adam.

She expresses disappointment,
anger, fear, and
finally, excitement.

Their first conversation triggers rejection.
Unfinished business from the past
has not been resolved.

Eve tries hard not to be judgmental.
She lets go of her need to answer
before Adam is finished.

Lighthearted Scene

But say, Adam, now we're alone.

Legendary Road Trip

At the highest point of desire,
Eve discerns with unprecedented clarity.

She becomes one with her purpose
and moves with power and precision.

Eve refuses to allow Adam to steal her peace.
She sets a watch for his shenanigans,

considers where she's been
and where she's headed,

makes countless course corrections
as devastation seems to rule the world.

A Thinker and Doer

Eve systematically winces
and amplifies content.

Her new life
a downward spiral.

She looks for a river
or stream

to quench her thirst.
The ugly truth

an aging body.
Like a sidewalk

in a dry desert
a clever cactus yards away

any man would run towards it,
any cactus will do.

Eve Flowers into Tenderness

An ample woman,
with great breasts,
she whispers of a new life.

Their laughter,
while changing, and rearranging every prop in sight,
only hints of despair.

The Unnamable Well

Eve finds herself at Mass
during the Consecration
thinking about the man in front of her.
She wonders if he's single.

Eve admits her guilt.
Stays away from
You make me . . .
and *You never . . .*

Apocalyptic Whisper

Product of the fall
and overwhelmed with terror,
Adam attempts to atone

scores lots of points.
His ambivalence is profound,
no more compulsion

to turn with the wind.
He declares absolute zero
or dive into randomness.

Eve puts emphasis
on where they ate,
throwing callous earth gods

speechless.
Adam sends a bottle
of Pinot Grigio

to the table.
Big
mistake.

Magnetic Lockbox

Now it takes preparation
to turn Adam on.

What to wear
and iron (or not)

the primping and positive tapes,
a shower.

Eve whips herself
into a frenzy.

She would chew off
her right arm for him.

Her as-if an exact replica
of her if-only.

Bickering About Pronouns

Eve feels useless.
She has no hobbies
or interests besides her family.

She keeps house, cooks,
does the laundry, sets out
Adam's clothes every morning.

She is lonely now that her children
are grown and living
on their own.

Adam encourages her
to take up writing.
He hints she seek counseling.

Metaphysical Leg-Pull

Like strangers
they wait

for comfortable feelings.
Chess and astrology occupy

Adam's mind.
They practice caring behavior:

a written message,
a simple I love you

whispered across a pillow.
Eve keeps a list of the things they've done.

No More Finger-Pointing

Eve takes time out,
stays away from button-pushing,

stops screaming
and walks away.

Adam suggests a movie,
helps her in with the groceries.

A Body and Soul Connection

Eve has let herself go.
Her figure has changed.
Her hair has grayed.
Adam's self-image is threatened.
He is determined to stay young.

Cain and Abel Arrange a Hot Air Balloon Ride

Adam and Eve see the world
in a new light.

They float in space
able to view their ranch

and surrounding areas.
They look at God's creation

and atone.
Their sex evolves.

Territorial Ground Rules

Get in here and clean up
your side of the room.

I'm getting the heck
out of here.

Clean up your own side
of the room

you little prick.
Cain picks up

one of his clodhoppers
to fling at his brother,

then he turns and punches
with all his strength.

Eve, who was reading
in her study,

looks to see
her two sons rush in.

He's freakin' crazy.
He attacked me!

I swear to God, Mom,
one day I'm going

to kill him.
I'm going to kill

both of you
if you don't knock it off.

Eve Plays the Role of Solomon

You two are just going to have to work this out on your own.

Innocence Lost

The Blackest Betrayal

A scorched scene,
where the serpent seeks
to die, still alive
on many levels at once,
begging at the door.

The soft and small and easily
preyed upon await
like spindly plants
for snake to insert his dagger,
then feel shame.

An anesthetic so effective,
carefully placed exotic rhododendrons,
liverworts and mosses
appear spontaneous
to the rest of the audience.

Woman Wearing Red Ruff Collar

Securely fastened cargo
and screaming, our
daughter's face
a scarlet berry.

Individual spaces,
intended for parking
motor vehicles, become
the backdrop and the plot.

He wears a drive-thru
body grin and waves
good-bye. I stand
erect under an autumn sky.

Mother Bathing Child

The water is warm
as I bathe her.

Like a spectator, I lean
over the porcelain tub.

She sits firm—tirelessly
cleaning the sides.

I begin spreading
soap like butter

on all the curves of her
white-bread body.

She shows me her
cuts and bruises

collected—proud
of her I acknowledge

each one. And
the mistaken freckle

that looks like dirt
to both of us.

Long Story Short

He kissed me hello
then each day thereafter
he insisted a little more
a little later

it was never the same.
A brutal affair.

You have no idea.

Watching him lift his glass,
watching him go down on me,

his bloodshot eyes
roll into his head.
His rough hands pull
my tight ass in.

Beyond the Silent Years

We were newlyweds
but I was not carried

with gentleness
to bed. I was drug

to the video store
in a strip mall

every Friday night.
His hard hand

gripped mine as he led
me down the center aisle

to the Adult Section.
We passed a display of staff picks,

dozens of melodramas.
I remember the historical

documentaries
and begging to go.

All Hallows Eve—A Series of Senryū

Senryū tend to be about human foibles while haiku tend to be about nature, and senryū are often cynical or darkly humorous while haiku are more serious. Unlike haiku, senryū do not include a kireji (cutting word), and do not generally include a kigo, or season word.

A Whisker
I need to forgive
like bristly hairs on a rat
the man I married

Two-Dimensional Cut-Out
Quiet as a grudge
even though I am crying
I apologize

More than a Miscarriage
Lips crack from release
to be someone's funeral
right there on the pot

Like an Unwelcome Guest
Under the table
a hollow ghost devours
complaints and breadcrumbs

New Moon Lament

Abrasive surface
gravitational flypaper
suddenly something

Cat Cries

I should have known by the crisp, cold air
the cats would be crying,
but it was the high-pitched growling
that woke me

It echoed my uneasy frustration,
the restless feeling
I hid so well during the day

What nonsense we live with,
the howling we disguise as living

I woke in absurdity to my alarm,
then rolled over
and for what, why I thought,
Why do we even get up?

I was in the grocery store earlier
carrying a basket on my arm,
my daughter trailing behind me
and I knocked over
a jar of marinara sauce

It went down my leg,
in-between my toes
and all over the floor,
broken glass was everywhere
I wanted to howl
I wanted to vanish

Smash racism and poverty
throw it away in large dumpsters
go bowling

to raise money for diabetes
walk an endless maze of roadway
to end sexual harassment

Pick a cause
and act on it
somebody somewhere
then go to sleep for God's sake

do something constructive:
move to New Mexico
buy an adobe home
raise Indian orphans in the name of the poor
go out to eat
and order Somalia steaks
real people food

The pitch of the cat cries
kept me on the edge of my bed
I clearly wasn't going back to sleep
outside, below my window
there could have been two, three or four cats
by the sound of it
the noise became lower and more primal
as the night grew colder and more absurd
my curtains were dancing
as the chilly air blew in
and one cat
was peeing on the fountain out back
claiming our yard his

The grass really grew in well this year

there are children who play there now
children who need clothes
who do not speak English yet
they talk in tongues
and they cry out at night in tongues
howl at night in tongues
But where do they pee?

On mountains of bones, I suppose,

in tin cups,
alleyways,
or in dumpsters
those babies don't know what sleep is
or what food feels like

I guess I'm lucky to be lying here
in my bed, in my room
even though the cats are pissing me off

why did they have to pick tonight to be in heat?

My daughter shit herself today
she had been playing outside
when she felt it coming

she ran in
and called to me
she was soaked
she had no footing
and she called to me

I came to find her standing
in her wet clothes
in the bathroom

She said she was sorry

I dropped to my knees
to wipe up
and while she showered
I waited

She said she was only dreaming
she said she did it on purpose

she told me she wants her Mommy and Daddy
to live together again

I can always catch up on sleep
some other time
I thought

I opened up a book
on how to write poems
and I read it through to the back
I wasn't angryanymore when I finished
the cats had stopped crying by then

But I kept hearing the children
their voices were in my head
so I leapt up from the bed
to the lower level of our house

I switched on the outside light
in hopes of saving a cat
perhaps I would see one in the window
or one on our front stoop

No cats

The book was done
and I was awake
it was hours till I'd have to wake to the alarm

Ether
makes you behave
in strange ways
like alcohol in excess
you can't see straight
you have no balance
and your tongue swells
you can't control yourself

All I could see

was the deep green silhouette
of the willow trees
that surround the back of our house

I turned to go back upstairs
and tripped
over a pile of toys

she hadn't put away before bed
I was twisted and demented

I was a sick woman by then
I didn't want to be sick
I didn't feel sick
but I was

my bathrobe was all bunched up
between my legs
my hair was a mess
and I started to babble insanely:

"A huge reptile was gnawing on a woman's neck,
the carpet was a blood-soaked sponge—impossible
to walk on, no footing at all"
I read from Hunter Thompson with fond memories of my youth
and being young
reliving those glory days of drugging myself
those snorting smoking fun-loving hitch-hiking acid tripping days
To the chorus of the cats and the wind
I read about America in the 70s
The pages turned
and I rolled over to sleep
She wet the bed that night
and the rug
and her pajamas
and the quilt

I came and found her standing

in her own soil
she said she was sorry

I dropped to my knees
to wipe up
and while she showered

I waited
and when she was done
I picked up

I switched on the outside light
to break up the cat fight
perhaps I would see one in the window
or one on our front stoop

I was wide awake then
it was hours till I'd have to wake to the alarm
I think there's something wrong with me
I can't get the crying out of my head

I hear those cats
and the children with no food
the sick
the abandoned
the dead
the fountain
the howling
the bed

I staggered towards the stairs
and slipped down
two flights of them
to find an empty window

No cats
I thought I may have been hearing things

I'm sorry Mommy
I didn't mean it

I won't do it again
I want you and Daddy to be together again
I did it on purpose

so I went bowling
I drove to the alley
on the corner of York and Fitzwatertown.

I put on those ugly shoes
and chose a large, heavy ball

I began to bowl for diabetes
I bowled and bowled until I was tired
tired of raising money for diseases
and sickness
when I wasn't sick
at least I didn't feel sick
but I really was
I was very, very sick

My daughter shit herself
before dinner she ran in
and called to me
when I found her
she was standing in her own soil
and she said sorry Mommy
and I dropped to my knees
to wipe up
and while she showered
I waited
and while she scrubbed herself

I picked up
and all the shit from the past
got all over me
and all over the bathroom
it just wouldn't go away
it just won't go away

In My Last Life

I think of her while on my hands
and obedient knees, bracing
for the familiar thrust, inward.

Our child still in my womb.
Me and the four-post
bed shaking.

Me and the yellow-
with-age wallpaper
coming apart at the seams.

Me and the unpolished
knob on the narrow
closet door

our gaping holes
no key
to be found.

Erasure

And there was blood.
I wanted to be closer to my dad
with alcohol.

Alcoholic

He was smoking.
I was smoking.
I wanted to be there.
It's a huge issue—
really deep.

I'm kind of like a runaway
with my understanding
and I think it's fabulous.

Eve Calls the Motor Club Man to Recharge
Her Battery

Wispy Thing

Take your place
in darkness
on the forest floor.

Bare the burden
of decomposing
vast amounts of dead wood.

Move at the pace
of a slug
and lack sex organs.

With no chifforobe,
high heels,
or negligee,

transform yourself
into a cluster
of exotic blossoms.

Adam Cracks the Whip

His pockets are stuffed
with bananas.
He eats, smokes and suffers
from hemorrhoids.

Adam speaks
from the lavatory
in clichés like
"We are made
in the image of God"
and "Trust me,"

while Eve munches
on turnips and dry biscuits,
going about her work.
She cleans house to music
and wiggles in between
sofa cushions
until she is exalted.

Nothing to Be Afraid of

Eve pretends
to live the role
of a hairdresser.
She wears skinny
blue jeans, a pale pink
smock and a stack
of glittery bracelets
that klink together
when she polishes
her nails,
cleans her gun,
and cuts
apples with cheese.

Eve stretches
her acting muscles
and courts the camera.
She sees the playback
on the monitor
and says, yes, I am
a Beautician!

To Be Woven into Garlands by Children

And so the sky sent down
to the corn and wheat fields

small glints of itself
in the form of flowers

dainty and feathery,
delightful and queer,

some ribbon-like,
others forked at the tips.

Bless those starry blue bells
with their wide reddish blue,

flower heads and odd
endearing faces.

Nymphomaniac

Eve uses sex to get attention
with few apparent rules
and a sense

of "enter into."
Adam no longer seeks
to escape it.

His 22-year-old days
behind him, he toils
determined to die in misery.

Soundstage

Eve gives a full
performance.

She shares outrageous
show biz gossip

in the Green Room,
but doesn't talk

about the audition
for fear she'll jinx it.

Nudity Required

Eve gives herself
permission

to be phenomenal.
She considers

low budget "B" movies.
Adam only agrees

to the use of a body double.
Eve is concerned

about the sacrifice
it takes to keep

her body
looking glorified.

The Day of Reckoning

Eve sees unshaven Adam
as a quirkish mirror
that reflects
her need to let go.

Now that Adam
is retired,
he wants to travel
but Eve is afraid
to fly.

Adam proposes
she get help
at the phobia clinic.
She refuses.

It's a standoff.

If Eve Had Her Life to Live Over

She would never
go anywhere
without her thermometer
and a parachute.

She would limber up,
be sillier
and start barefoot
earlier in spring.

The Right Amount of Sunshine and Water

Eve is not enamored
with hot flashes
and a full bladder
in the middle of the night.

She oscillates
between two extremes:
she either pretends
to be loving
or not.

Eve Strives to Become an Opera Singer

She descends and stabilizes
while wading
in the Jordan River.

Nature wraps itself
around woman and bells ring.
Eve decides to renew herself

by purchasing
a ringed binder
with divider sections.

Her dividers are labeled
mind, body and soul.
She envisions

her life a gigantic puzzle
with missing pieces.
She constructs

a circle with strokes
that radiate like brilliant candles,
then tries to write a short story.

The Final Act Opens

The apple tree sports
a few new leaves
but nothing has changed.

The curtain rises.

Backstroke

A Journal of True Confessions

"Want some porridge?" I asked her.
"No," she replied.

There's this diner she likes,
that serves scrapple and eggs
on porcelain dishes,
and the waitresses wear badges.

"I know how to cook scrapple,"
I said.

On her bed,
we talked about morning foods,
like cereal and muffins
and the smell of porridge trailed
up the corridor
wrapping around doorways
and into the room.

"I think cereal
is like a breakfast shortcut."

"Why won't you eat porridge?" I asked her.
"Because I'm not a bear," she said,
"and I hate cereal."

"Well, you're having it."
"But I hate it."

"It's easy."

"It's boring."

"It's good for you, and you're going to eat it."

I always feel better when I exert my maternal authority,
like I'm doing what I should,
like I'm being a real mom.
Maybe I should wear a badge.

When the porridge cools,
we will eat

until we are full,
and that will make me happy.
The clouds pushed away from the sky,
and the morning sun trickled in
window shade's filtered shadows
dancing like little wall-silhouettes.

A flash of light.
A puff of smoke.
We remembered the bad dream.

Sometimes my voice
echoes in my head.
I know I told her not to go into the woods,
not to go,
I said.

"Do not
take the shortcut through the forest.
I've heard that
bears live there."

It was a stormy night,
and she woke yelling, "Mommy, I'm scared!"

From what I could gather, Martha was this larger-than-life creature
who was chasing her,
and she was running for her life.

"Martha was chasing me.
She was wearing a blue dress
with white buttons running down
the front of a house
with white buttons
running in the woods."

Wasn't it the wolf that said, "What big eyes you have!"
but your ears,
they're so small.
"Didn't you hear your Mother?"
"I didn't get the muffins, Mom."

"You went through the woods."

"Yes."

"Why."

"I don't know. How did you know?"

I always wondered how my mother always knew everything, too.

It was dark.
I was lying alone in my bed.
She burst in

pleading to sleep with me.
I said, "No—
sleep in your own bed."

The room was still
and the moon shone through
the window shade's filtered shadows
dancing like little wall-silhouettes.

I tucked her back into her own small bed.

When morning came
I woke with fury
to find her next to me
in my bed.

"Somebody's been lying in my bed," I cried.

"I couldn't sleep," she said.

Our eyes met,
the wind blew the chill of the dream
over us again,
and we huddled together.

"Want some porridge?" I asked.

"No," she replied.
"I want to go to the diner."

Your Body Is Changing

The shape of you
grows round and square
while mine diminishes
in your shadow.

Your hairy legs
remind me
it's time to explain
the deep significance
of sharp edged things.

Believe by Degrees

The night of the big show
the music was strong
and methodical.
The conductor stood tall.

How he moved you
to the back row
because your fluted skirt
was in short measure.

How the fifth position
seat you earned vanished
into the sharp space
of your open legs.

How you learned
to position your shoulders
parallel with the stage
ankles crossed like Jesus.

The Social Fabric

ABOUT THE AUTHOR
Watching television all my life
has led me to believe
in dis-ease.

COMMODITY
The uniform people,
the sellers
in gray linen,
must tell the truth in advertising
otherwise
our rational decision-making
process
becomes seriously impaired.

PRINCESS
I saw Pocahontas
on the street corner
wearing flowers like beads
around her neck.
An authentic object
she was
eating a mustard sandwich.
I stood blind.
She turned to me
as if to say,
if there were people before us
how did they come?
I would have replied,
they were born, like us,
if she had asked.

COMMERCIAL
"What?" said Joseph.
"What'd you say?" said Mary.
"Jesus, I said 'What.' "

SUBWAY
A crowd of people nodded
sleepwalking and threadbare
every thread a sign
Pocahontas began unraveling
the fabric.

IT WAS GETTING DARK
"Can you touch the sky?"
she asked me.
I said, "Only in your dreams."
Pocahontas asked what a dream was.
I said, "It's when you are asleep
and you see something."
She hesitated,
then asked, "WHERE DO THEY GO?"
"Everywhere," I told her,
"everywhere."

5:45 a.m.   My alarm sounds.
             I press snooze.
6:05 a.m.   My alarm sounds again,
             and I get up.
6:40   I wake Julie Anne.
6:45   I prepare breakfast.
7:05   We eat together,
7:20   get dressed,

7:25   brush our teeth, and
7:40   we head out,
          saying to each other that each of us
          loves the other,
          wishing we really didn't have to go,
          knowing that leaving is the hardest part of being human.
7:45   I drive away,
          and she walks to the bus stop.

STATIC
She told me once
she never feels alone
so long as
there is a picture of me
near her,
that pictures aren't alive
but can think and see and feel,
then her eyes filled with tears.

COMMERCIAL
"What?" said Joseph.
"What'd you say?" said Mary.
"Jesus, I said 'What.'"

STIPULATION
I thought to myself
this job is large.
I have undertaken the unconscious
mass of human flesh—
leery of truth.

Instant Therapy + 5 Cents = Hypothetical Example

Examples of this kind
are hard to create,
because it is difficult
to make hypothetical examples
plausible.
They do, however,
play an important role
in your arsenal
of supporting material.

COMMERCIAL
"What?" said Joseph.
"What'd you say?" said Mary.
"Jesus, I said 'What.' "

ABOUT THE AUTHOR
Sometimes when I think
how TV
has affected my life,
I realize
I was silenced by it.
I made my food to the tunes of supermarket jingles,
and now I train my daughter
to be silent, too,
to stare with complacency.

6:15 p.m.   SPLASH
               I fill the pot with water,
               set it on the stove to boil,
               reach up
               for a box of macaroni.

110

7:45 p.m.   RELAX
We're lying together
on her bed.
She is reading to me.
I'm thinking it's incredible to be human.

SIDEWALK
Pocahontas looked down,
her eyes met her feet.
Her feet were bare.
I watched
litter blowing along the street.
I heard a siren going off
and there were cars,
lots of cars.

TRAFFIC
No Parking signs,
abandoned vehicles,
caution
written across the faces of everyone.

A TV REPAIRMAN SHOUTED
from his van window,
"Being sold solutions is better than
being confronted
with questions and problems."

POETRY
This would be the last time Pocahontas and I found our faces
looking squarely
at each other.
Places we had been
gone.

REFRAIN
Human-Human-Human Being
Being-Being-Being Human

COMMERCIAL
"What?" said Joseph.
"What'd you say?" said Mary.
"Jesus, I said 'What.' "

JOKE
So, Julie Anne says to me
in the foreseeable future,
"You know, Mom,
even the earliest cave paintings
were only visual projections
of the hunt.
They were just wish fulfillments
that inspired the hunter."

SHOCK
I faint.
She calls an ambulance.

911
"Mom," she yells.
"Will you sit with me and watch TV?"

"What?"

Back Stroke

Floating
no, gliding
across the river
no, pool of sea

her body in all its
glory, no
eloquence
and her two budding

breasts
peeking out atop
the shimmering
no, rippling crystal blanket.

The Winner Is…
Eve at the Academy Awards

Wanderlust

When all danger
of frost is past,

dig and prepare
for seeding.

Spade the earth,
remove roots and rocks.

After shaking off
still-clinging dirt,

toss out sod and keep
vigil for seedlings.

Their twin, pale-green leaves
will push through

the ground and you
will have plenty.

Eve Glances at Her Reflection
in the Sea of Galilee

What once was creamy
smooth and flawless
is now the face
of a fifty-year-old.

She looks for answers,
stacks a deck
of tarot cards
and whirls to face her future.

Eve Fixes Her Attention on Nirvana

Adam articulates a few
last words from his heart.

An aura of lingering
is everywhere.

Eve dilly-dallies
down a country road

to meet him
at the railway station.

The bypass bustles
with cars and bikes.

She appears bouncy
and open like the road.

The Paradox

Although Eve was made
from his rib,

she wants a role of her own.
To be a clown balancing

spinning plates. Her thirst
for independence, a fire pristine.

Fire and Ice

Adam is compelled
to find pleasure

in the inevitable dead end.
Eve is commissioned

to dramatize a sweeping city scene.
Adam scoffs at the idea.

Between Mud and Stars

Eve spins a net
of images and her heart

is torn from her chest.
A new one is put in

which invokes euphoria.
Farewell to all valiant efforts

and pitying.
So long unforgiving creatures!

Sayonara street of sought
to escape it!

Aloha, everybody! Here's to the raw,
and the rough.

Her star now apart from the galaxy
of shadows.

With her eyes shut tight, she is
animal grace in a new jungle world.

Eve Walks Through an Open Door

Like an appointed archer,
Her exalted arrow
Marks the target.

Red light.
Camera rolling.

She Claims It Frees Her

The work of an artist
and the blood
red as a whore's child
being beaten

at the school yard.
Imagine
being young again
and how it feels.

You know when to stop.
You know when to slow down.
While in word thoughts,
her child stays,

kept far away
from her habit.
The mother
of a red child,

Mother
with no cookies baking,
not a shred
of clean clothing,

and red because of it.
Though she reads
books of poetry,
her own maroon thoughts,

she claims it frees her
it will never leave her

she is lost,
left dreaming

when she should be baking
and washing away stains.
The child
will learn to love
the color red.

For one day,

she will bleed, too
all women do,

their blood
their only mark:
word whores
with well-read children.

I Have. I am. I Thought I'd Die. But I Didn't.

Two radiating bodies
posed, facing each other
in the open air.
The space surrounding
them cleared of things.
Figure 1 seeks
the orbit of Figure 2
not fully grown.

Both exposed
wearing the same clothes
looking indistinguishable
from one another
like little bits of vivified
matter trying to stand
their ground. Figure 1 gently
touches the slope of
shoulder with affection

and says,
"This is what you are to me."

Pulling for the Heroine

[Eve leaps off the stage.
Adam is paralyzed.]

Eve: (Quietly) Is it time?
Adam: (Looking nervously at the apple) Not yet.
Eve: Don't be afraid.
Adam: But God said…
Eve: Shhhh.

About the Author

An advocate for creative writing and community service, Joanne Leva is founder and Executive Director of the Montgomery County, Pennsylvania, Poet Laureate Program (MCPL).

Her poems have appeared in *The American Poetry Review, Peace Is a Haiku Song* (The Foundry Books), *50 Over Fifty* (PS Books), *Schuylkill Valley Journal, Mad Poet's Review, The Bucks County Writer, Transcendent Visions, The Souderton Independent,* and John Timpane's Entertainment – Arts blog at philly.com.

Leva's poem, "Looking Back on the Mountain," was featured in an exhibition and companion publication entitled, *Making Magic: Beauty in Word and Image* at the James A. Michener Museum in Doylestown, Pennsylvania (November 2012 through March 2013).

Joanne has organized poetry readings at the Souderton Art Jam for *100 Thousand Poets for Change,* Headhouse Square for Earth Day, the Seven Arts Fest on South Street, The Theater of Living Arts, The Philadelphia Museum of Art, The James A. Michener Museum, The Mutter Museum, World Café, The Login Inn, Ambler Theater, Barnes & Noble Booksellers, and Farley's Bookshop.

Follow her on social media at #evewouldknow

www.ingramcontent.com/pod-product-compliance
Lightning Source LLC
Chambersburg PA
CBHW071825090426
42737CB00012B/2187